There is so much to admire about a little life which brings light to everything in its path. ☀

~Sharon

Bebe, the Fairy of Light

Written and Illustrated by Sharon Knotts Hass

Copyright @2022 by (Sharon Knotts Hass)

All rights reserved. No part of this book may be reproduced in any form or by any electronic or mechanical means, including information storage and retrieval systems, without permission in writing from the publisher, except by reviewers, who may quote brief passages in a review.

This publication contains the opinions and ideas of its author. It is intended to provide helpful and informative material on the subjects addressed in the publication. The author and publisher specifically disclaim all responsibility for any liability, loss or risk, personal or otherwise, which is incurred as a consequence, directly or indirectly, of the use and application of any of the contents of this book.

WORKBOOK PRESS LLC
187 E Warm Springs Rd,
Suite B285, Las Vegas, NV 89119, USA

Website: https://workbookpress.com/
Hotline: 1-888-818-4856
Email: admin@workbookpress.com

Ordering Information:
Quantity sales. Special discounts are available on quantity purchases by corporations, associations, and others. For details, contact the publisher at the address above.

Library of Congress Control Number:
ISBN-13: 978-1-957618-24-1 (Paperback Version)
978-1-957618-25-8 (Digital Version)

REV. DATE: 01/26/2022

Dedication

For my granddaughter Deanne "Bebe".

Love you, Gramz

The sun was rising in the valley.

Bebe stretched and yawned then smiled. She has a lot of places to visit and things to see, off she goes.

There are a lot of beautiful flowers to smell.

There are ladybugs to pet, songbirds to hear and warm sunshine to feel.

You see in this particular valley,
most fairies come out at night, but not Bebe, she prefers the warm, bright sunlight.

In the big Hawthorn tree at the river's end,
Belle, Lindsey, Katrina and Fay, Bebe's fairy friends, all sleep the day away.

On her own, she flies through the gardens searching for the butterflies. Her favorite is Kristen she is red, white and blue with pretty green eyes. Bebe says hello then flies along to her next destination.

There is a river, a field of flowers and grass of green.
Colors of pink, blue and yellow with purple and white in between. Bebe flies upside down and all around.

This beautiful scenery is what Bebe can't resist. She thought of the beauty her friends have all missed. The bees with their honey so sweet, it is such a yummy treat.

The birds in their nests and all the rest. There is just so much to see.

There is her friend Freddie the Frog by a Lilly, he is always acting very silly. He is waiting for his friend Alexander the Toad who is hopping along by the road. Bebe waves a big hi as she flies through the sky.

Bebe's favorite turtle Tootles is taking his time, he is on his way to eat grapes from a vine. Conner the caterpillar is going to stay by the grape leaves for the day. Bebe says hello to them from up above.

Among the tulips Bebe felt the sunshine on her face.
The tulip patch is her favorite place.

Much to her surprise, Bebe's friends came to play! They told her how wonderful it is and that they plan to be awake during the day. They talked about their adventure for a while. This happy news made Bebe smile.

Everything she touches become a little more bright.
That is because Bebe is the fairy of light.

Bebe gives thanks to God for another good day.

www.ingramcontent.com/pod-product-compliance
Lightning Source LLC
Chambersburg PA
CBHW041429080526
44579CB00021B/51